# ROLL-A-PROMPT WRITING JUMPSTARTS

## SCENE EDITION

ROLL-A-PROMPT
BOOK 8

MELISSA BANCZAK

LISA MAHONEY

GROOVY QUILL, LLC

Copyright © 2023 by Melissa Banczak and Lisa Mahoney

All rights reserved.

No part of this book may be reproduced in any form or by any electronic or mechanical means, including information storage and retrieval systems, without written permission from the author, except for the use of brief quotations in a book review.

❦ Created with Vellum

# CONTENTS

| | |
|---|---|
| About the Authors | vi |
| Also by the Authors | vii |
| Why we Wrote This Book | viii |
| How to Use This Book | ix |
| 10 Free Prompts! | x |
| Dice Pattern | xi |
| | |
| Hobby Farm | 1 |
| Boutique | 7 |
| Cruise Ship | 13 |
| Marina | 19 |
| Underground Altar | 25 |
| Psychiatric Hospital | 31 |
| Mountain Top | 37 |
| Cellar | 43 |
| Carnival | 49 |
| Art Gallery | 55 |
| Penthouse Apartment | 61 |
| Desert | 67 |
| Freak Show | 73 |
| Museum | 79 |
| Cafeteria | 85 |
| Broadway Theater | 91 |
| Car Dealership | 97 |
| Abandoned Railway Station | 103 |
| Bar | 109 |
| Funeral Home | 115 |
| Cave | 121 |
| Emergency Room | 127 |
| Library | 133 |
| Church Crypt | 139 |
| School Campus | 145 |
| A Warehouse | 151 |
| Camp Site | 157 |
| Nightclub | 163 |

Cooking Class 169
Nursing Home 175

Also by the Authors 181

*Melissa -*
*Smoochous to Mark*

*Lisa -*
*For David who makes me laugh every day (and who would kill me if I sent him smoochous)*

ABOUT THE AUTHORS

In another lifetime, Melissa Banczak was an editor, ghost writer and literary agent specializing in screenplays. She writes the June Nash Mystery series and has a podcast called Books Cubed where she interviews the indie authors you should be reading. Her favorite games involve dice.

In this lifetime, Lisa Mahoney is an award-winning short story writer, English professor, and most importantly a dreamer. She hides her secret happiness when the power goes out and the generator won't work and her family is forced to play board games with her. She has just completed her first novel.

**Roll-A-Prompt Writing Journal Series**

**Genre Editions:**

- Mystery
- Horror
- Sci-Fi
- Romance
- Fantasy
- Genre Mashup
- More Coming 2023

**Story Building Editions:**

- Conflict
- Scene
- Five Senses
- More Coming 2023

For updates on new Roll-A-Prompt Writing Journals and periodic live writing prompt sessions, join our community when you download your free PDF worksheets at: https://BookHip.com/FZHMZA

## WHY WE WROTE THIS BOOK

Writers have imaginations. We play the *what-if* and *I-wonder-whether* games that make many of the realists around us scrunch up their noses. But sometimes we get stuck and our imaginations need to find a side door or a backdoor or even a trapdoor—a new way in to our stories. Once in, there's no telling where our creativity will take us. But how do we find those hidden passageways and allay our *stuckness*?

Many depend on prompt books. We're no different yet we yearned to have a *different approach*. So in our efforts to jumpstart our own writing and fire up our fantasies, we turned to our love of games and the randomness of dice and the Roll-A-Prompt Series was born.

Use it alone or with friends. With over 6000 possible combinations, it's the perfect way to get your creative juices flowing.

*Melissa & Lisa*

## HOW TO USE THIS BOOK

Each Roll-A-Prompt Edition features 30 sets of elements that, with the roll of a dice, will create over 6000 prompts per book. What you'll need:

- Pen or pencil
- Dice (pattern included in the PDF)
- Imagination

Roll for your prompt. Jot it all down at the top of a work page. Let your imagination run wild.

A *late woman* doesn't always have to be someone running behind. She could also be pregnant. Or dead.

A *pizza delivery driver* is not just a job designation. It's also a treasure trove of stuff. They'd probably have a car. A phone. Some pizza. Use what you want. It's your prompt.

Want to get even more out of this book? Turn to a random page for your scene. Then another for your first element. Another for your second. A third for the last. Voila! A new prompt.

So roll your dice, get writing, and above all, have fun!

*Melissa & Lisa*

*We'd love to know how the prompts worked out for you. Did you start a story? Finish one? Publish? Did you try this with your writing group? Email us at mel@melissabanczak.com*

10 FREE PROMPTS!

Be a part of our writing community and get a free monthly prompt!

Type the link below into your browser for a PDF with:

- 10 additional free prompts
- A lined work page
- A dice pattern to print, cutout, and tape together
- An opportunity to join Melissa and Lisa for live writing prompt sessions on the Books Cubed Podcast.

It's free and you can unsubscribe at any time.

https://dl.bookfunnel.com/do6l14xo66

Hope you can join us,
*Melissa & Lisa*

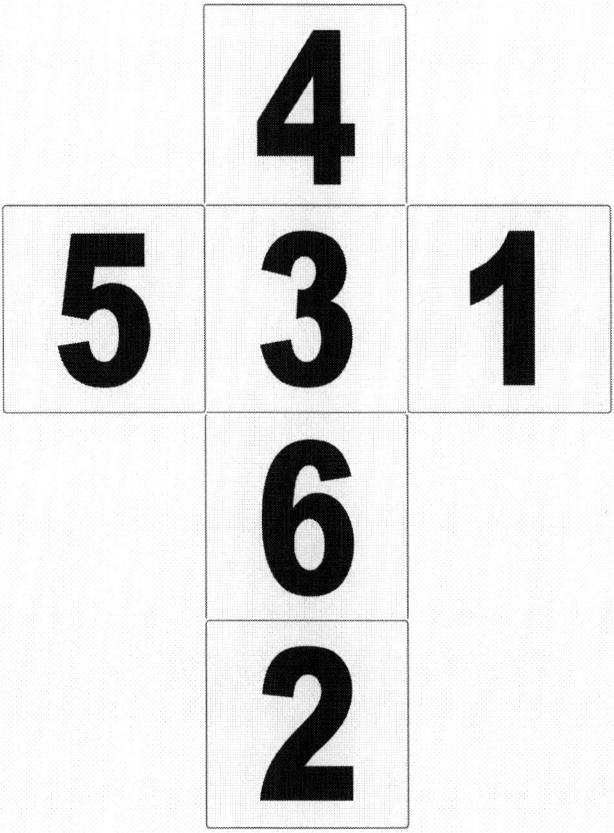
4
5 3 1
6
2

## The setting is a Hobby Farm. Write one scene.

**Roll for Climate:**

- Odd - Northern State with Winter
- Even - Southern State always Sunshine

**Roll for Product:**

1. Goat Milk Soap
2. Ostrich Meat
3. Alpaca Fiber
4. Eggs
5. Bees
6. Buffalo Teeth

**Roll for Adjective:**

1. Judgemental
2. Jubilant
3. Juicy
4. Jovial
5. Jaundiced
6. Jocular

**Roll for Time of Day:**

- Odd - Daytime
- Even - Nighttime

# ROLL-A-PROMPT WRITING JUMPSTARTS

Climate_____ Product_____
Adjective_____Time_____

HOBBY FARM

Climate_____ Product_____
Adjective_____ Time_____

## ROLL-A-PROMPT WRITING JUMPSTARTS

Climate_____ Product_____
Adjective_____ Time_____

HOBBY FARM

Climate_____ Product_____
Adjective_____ Time_____

ROLL-A-PROMPT WRITING JUMPSTARTS

Climate_____ Product_____
Adjective_____Time_____

<u>The setting is a Boutique. Write one scene.</u>

**Roll for MC's Nickname:**

1. Tiny
2. Petal
3. Bear
4. Kitty
5. Bumper
6. Honey

**Roll for Animal:**

1. Snake
2. Fox
3. Emu
4. Hummingbird
5. Ant Eater
6. Raccoon

**Roll for Word:**

1. Bushwack
2. Thwonk
3. Disembark
4. Flank
5. Interlock
6. Recaulk

**Roll for Shop's Status:**

- Odd - Open
- Even - Closed

**Roll for Number of Shop's Occupants.** Use What Comes Up On Your Dice.

ROLL-A-PROMPT WRITING JUMPSTARTS

Nickname_____ Animal_____ Word_____
Status_____Number of Characters_____

BOUTIQUE

Nickname_____ Animal_____ Word_____
Status_____ Number of Characters_____

ROLL-A-PROMPT WRITING JUMPSTARTS

Nickname_____ Animal_____ Word_____
Status_____Number of Characters_____

BOUTIQUE

Nickname_____ Animal_____ Word_____
Status_____Number of Characters_____

ROLL-A-PROMPT WRITING JUMPSTARTS

Nickname_____ Animal_____ Word_____
Status_____Number of Characters_____

<u>The setting is a Cruise Ship. Write one scene.</u>

**Roll for Character:**

1. Dancer
2. Chef
3. Widow/Widower
4. Activities Director
5. Lifeguard
6. Newlywed

**Roll for Adjective:**

1. Dear
2. Ubiquitous
3. Clever
4. Narrow
5. Burly
6. Lying

**Roll for Food:**

1. Bananas Foster
2. Octopus
3. Breadsticks
4. Steak Tar-Tar
5. Nachos
6. Poutine

ROLL-A-PROMPT WRITING JUMPSTARTS

Character_____ Adjective_____
Food_____

CRUISE SHIP

Character_____ Adjective_____
Food_____

ROLL-A-PROMPT WRITING JUMPSTARTS

Character_____ Adjective_____
Food_____

CRUISE SHIP

Character_____ Adjective_____
Food_____

ROLL-A-PROMPT WRITING JUMPSTARTS

Character_____ Adjective_____
Food_____

<u>The setting is a Marina. Write one scene.</u>

**Roll for Character:**

1. Stripper
2. Teacher
3. Felon
4. Census Taker
5. Tax Preparer
6. Vegetarian

**Roll for Line of Dialog:**

1. I'm your grandchild.
2. Why do you have to argue?
3. You have to leave right now.
4. Did you see the ripples?
5. It was like that when I found it.
6. Is it in the bucket?

**Roll for Word:**

1. Trifle
2. Congestion
3. Thinktank
4. Pleasure
5. Solar
6. Hyperventilate

**Roll for Mood:**

- Odd - Tipsy
- Even - Somber

ROLL-A-PROMPT WRITING JUMPSTARTS

Character_____Dialog_____
Word_____Mood_____

MARINA

Character_____Dialog_____
Word_____Mood_____

ROLL-A-PROMPT WRITING JUMPSTARTS

Character_____Dialog_____
Word_____Mood_____

MARINA

Character_____Dialog_____
Word_____Mood_____

ROLL-A-PROMPT WRITING JUMPSTARTS

Character_____Dialog_____
Word_____Mood_____

## The setting is an Underground Altar. Write one scene.

**Roll for MC's Nickname:**

1. Sparky
2. Chicky
3. Fishlips
4. Rooster
5. Whiffer
6. Cookie

**Roll for Dilemma:**

1. Cellphone Keeps Ringing and Disconnecting
2. Temperature is Rising
3. Short Term Memory Loss
4. Map Gets Destroyed
5. Key Doesn't Work in Lock
6. A Noise is Getting Closer and Closer

**Roll for Verb:**

1. Grin
2. Recon
3. Weaken
4. Regain
5. Summon
6. Ban

ROLL-A-PROMPT WRITING JUMPSTARTS

Nickname_____ Dilemma_____
Verb_____

UNDERGROUND ALTAR

Nickname_____ Dilemma_____
Verb_____

ROLL-A-PROMPT WRITING JUMPSTARTS

Nickname_____ Dilemma_____
Verb_____

UNDERGROUND ALTAR

Nickname_____ Dilemma_____
Verb_____

## ROLL-A-PROMPT WRITING JUMPSTARTS

Nickname_____ Dilemma_____
Verb_____

## The setting is a Psychiatric Hospital. Write one scene.

**Roll for MC's Status:**

- Odd - Patient
- Even - On Staff

**Roll for Verb:**

1. Scrunch
2. Encroach
3. Flinch
4. Entrench
5. Poach
6. Quench

**Roll for Food:**

1. Milkshake
2. Eggroll
3. Strawberry
4. Oatmeal Cookie
5. Avocado
6. Wedge of Cheese

**Roll for Section of Hospital:**

1. Padded Cell
2. Dormitory
3. Activities Room
4. Basement
5. Treatment Room
6. Kitchen

ROLL-A-PROMPT WRITING JUMPSTARTS

Status_____Verb_____
Food_____Section_____

PSYCHIATRIC HOSPITAL

Status_____Verb_____
Food_____Section_____

ROLL-A-PROMPT WRITING JUMPSTARTS

Status_____Verb_____
Food_____Section_____

PSYCHIATRIC HOSPITAL

Status_____Verb_____
Food_____Section_____

ROLL-A-PROMPT WRITING JUMPSTARTS

Status_____Verb_____
Food_____Section_____

<u>The setting is a Mountain Top. Write one scene.</u>

**Roll for Number of MC's Companions.** Use What Comes Up On Your Dice.

**Roll for Insect:**

1. Bumble Bee
2. Lice
3. Beetle
4. Ticks
5. Mud Dauber
6. Bed Bugs

**Roll for Article of Clothing:**

1. Apron
2. Corset
3. Garter Belt
4. Argyle Socks
5. Necktie
6. Crossing Guard Vest

**Roll for Color:**

1. Crimson
2. Vermilion
3. Alabaster
4. Periwinkle
5. Butterscotch
6. Jade

ROLL-A-PROMPT WRITING JUMPSTARTS

Companions_____Insect_____
Clothing_____Color_____

MOUNTAIN TOP

Companions_____Insect_____
Clothing_____Color_____

ROLL-A-PROMPT WRITING JUMPSTARTS

Companions_____Insect_____
Clothing_____Color_____

MOUNTAIN TOP

Companions_____Insect_____
Clothing_____Color_____

## ROLL-A-PROMPT WRITING JUMPSTARTS

Companions_____Insect_____
Clothing_____Color_____

## The setting is a Cellar. Write one scene.

**Roll for Number of MC's Companions.** Use What Comes Up On Your Dice.

**Roll for Mood:**

- Odd - Tense
- Even - Relaxed

**Roll for Line of Dialog:**

1. I never noticed before.
2. Are you jealous?
3. I'm still learning.
4. Can you hold this for me?
5. I'll show you why.
6. Did you get the letter?

**Roll for Event:**

1. Christmas
2. Thanksgiving
3. Halloween
4. Valentine's Day
5. Birthday
6. Funeral

ROLL-A-PROMPT WRITING JUMPSTARTS

Companions_____Mood_____
Dialog_____Event_____

CELLAR

Companions_____Mood_____
Dialog_____Event_____

ROLL-A-PROMPT WRITING JUMPSTARTS

Companions_____Mood_____
Dialog_____Event_____

CELLAR

Companions_____Mood_____
Dialog_____Event_____

ROLL-A-PROMPT WRITING JUMPSTARTS

Companions_____Mood_____
Dialog_____Event_____

## The setting is a Carnival. Write one scene.

**Roll for MC's Nickname:**

1. Scrappy
2. Buster
3. Thrasher
4. Molasses
5. Valentino
6. Chucklehead

**Roll for Dilemma:**

1. Missing Person
2. Flat Tire
3. Lost Wallet
4. Sudden Thunderstorm
5. Mysterious Rash
6. Electrical Fire

**Roll for Verb:**

1. Absorb
2. Disturb
3. Rub
4. Comb
5. Mob
6. Succumb

## ROLL-A-PROMPT WRITING JUMPSTARTS

Nickname_____ Dilemma_____
Verb_____

CARNIVAL

Nickname_____ Dilemma_____
Verb_____

ROLL-A-PROMPT WRITING JUMPSTARTS

Nickname_____ Dilemma_____
Verb_____

CARNIVAL

Nickname_____ Dilemma_____
Verb_____

ROLL-A-PROMPT WRITING JUMPSTARTS

Nickname_____ Dilemma_____
Verb_____

## The setting is an Art Gallery. Write one scene.

**Roll for MC's Participation:**

- Odd - Artist
- Even - Collector

**Roll for Type of Art:**

1. Sculpture
2. Nude Paintings
3. Chalk Art
4. Performance Art
5. Fashion
6. Photography

**Roll for Line of Dialog:**

1. Do you deny it?
2. Furry ones are the best.
3. Are there little seeds?
4. The switch is blue.
5. Why are you smiling?
6. They want to finish.

**Roll for Verb:**

1. Ambush
2. Belch
3. Froth
4. Inch
5. Perch
6. Flush

## ROLL-A-PROMPT WRITING JUMPSTARTS

Participation_____Art_____
Dialog_____Verb_____

ART GALLERY

Participation_____Art_____
Dialog_____Verb_____

ROLL-A-PROMPT WRITING JUMPSTARTS

Participation_____Art_____
Dialog_____Verb_____

ART GALLERY

Participation_____Art_____
Dialog_____Verb_____

_____
_____
_____
_____
_____
_____
_____
_____
_____
_____
_____
_____
_____
_____
_____
_____
_____
_____
_____
_____
_____
_____
_____
_____
_____
_____
_____
_____
_____
_____
_____
_____
_____
_____
_____
_____
_____

## ROLL-A-PROMPT WRITING JUMPSTARTS

Participation_____Art_____
Dialog_____Verb_____

## The setting is a Penthouse. Write one scene.

**Roll for MC's Visitor:**

1. Housekeeping
2. Food Delivery
3. Date
4. Door Attendant
5. Interior Designer
6. Therapist

**Roll for Kitchen Gadget:**

1. Apple Corer
2. Strawberry Huller
3. Electric Salt Grinder
4. Vacuum Sealer
5. Wire whisk
6. Compost Bin

**Roll for Animal:**

1. Iguana
2. Capybara
3. Tarantula
4. Hedgehog
5. Mini Pig
6. Sugar Glider

ROLL-A-PROMPT WRITING JUMPSTARTS

Visitor_____
Gadget_____Animal_____

PENTHOUSE APARTMENT

Visitor_____
Gadget_____Animal_____

ROLL-A-PROMPT WRITING JUMPSTARTS

Visitor_____
Gadget_____Animal_____

PENTHOUSE APARTMENT

Visitor_____
Gadget_____Animal_____

## ROLL-A-PROMPT WRITING JUMPSTARTS

Visitor_____
Gadget_____Animal_____

## The setting is the Desert. Write one scene.

**Roll for MC's Nickname:**

1. Snowflake
2. Moe
3. Scout
4. Nugget
5. Fink
6. Jinx

**Roll for Dilemma:**

1. Crack in the Water Bottle
2. Unrecognizable Animal in Distance
3. Separated from Group
4. Exhaustion Due to Heat stroke or Hypothermia
5. Compass Malfunction
6. Encampment is Thrashed

**Roll for Verb:**

1. Toss
2. Witness
3. Surpress
4. Kiss
5. Impress
6. Confess

ROLL-A-PROMPT WRITING JUMPSTARTS

Nickname_____ Dilemma_____
Verb_____

DESERT

Nickname_____ Dilemma_____
Verb_____

ROLL-A-PROMPT WRITING JUMPSTARTS

Nickname_____ Dilemma_____
Verb_____

DESERT

Nickname_____ Dilemma_____
Verb_____

ROLL-A-PROMPT WRITING JUMPSTARTS

Nickname_____ Dilemma_____
Verb_____

## The setting is a Freak Show. Write one scene.

**Roll for Event:**

1. Fortune Teller
2. Big Top
3. Fire Breather
4. Sword Swallower
5. Midway
6. Concessions

**Roll for Era:**

- Odd - Modern
- Even - Old Timey

**Roll for MC's Participation:**

- Odd - Attendee
- Even - Carny

**Roll for Word:**

1. Bumfuzzle
2. Cattywampus
3. Flummoxed
4. Gardyloo
5. Taradiddle
6. Lollygag

# ROLL-A-PROMPT WRITING JUMPSTARTS

Event_____Era_____
Participation_____Word_____

_____
_____
_____
_____
_____
_____
_____
_____
_____
_____
_____
_____
_____
_____
_____
_____
_____
_____
_____
_____
_____
_____
_____
_____
_____
_____
_____
_____
_____
_____
_____
_____
_____
_____

FREAK SHOW

Event_____Era_____
Participation_____Word_____

_____
_____
_____
_____
_____
_____
_____
_____
_____
_____
_____
_____
_____
_____
_____
_____
_____
_____
_____
_____
_____
_____
_____
_____
_____
_____
_____
_____
_____
_____
_____
_____

## ROLL-A-PROMPT WRITING JUMPSTARTS

Event_____Era_____
Participation_____Word_____

FREAK SHOW

Event_____Era_____
Participation_____Word_____

## ROLL-A-PROMPT WRITING JUMPSTARTS

Event_____Era_____
Participation_____Word_____

## The setting is a Museum. Write one scene.

**Roll for MC's Vocation:**

1. Tour Guide
2. Expert
3. Maintenance
4. Front Office
5. Security
6. Patron

**Roll for Museum's Status:**

- Odd - Closed
- Even - Open

**Roll for Exhibit:**

1. Dinosaurs
2. Meteorites
3. Ancient Civilization
4. Taxidermy
5. Aviation
6. Gems

**Roll for Unexpected Distraction:**

1. Email
2. Phone Message
3. Letter
4. Package
5. Visitor
6. Intercom

ROLL-A-PROMPT WRITING JUMPSTARTS

Vocation_____Status_____
Exhibit_____Distraction_____

MUSEUM

Vocation_____Status_____
Exhibit_____Distraction_____

ROLL-A-PROMPT WRITING JUMPSTARTS

Vocation_____Status_____
Exhibit_____Distraction_____

MUSEUM

Vocation_____Status_____
Exhibit_____Distraction_____

ROLL-A-PROMPT WRITING JUMPSTARTS

Vocation_____Status_____
Exhibit_____Distraction_____

## The setting is a Cafeteria. Write one scene.

**Roll for Character:**

1. Fashionista
2. Exhausted Individual
3. Bully
4. Janitor
5. Delivery Driver
6. Journalist

**Roll for Dilemma:**

1. No Condiments
2. Cash Register is Empty
3. Spilled Sugar on Floor
4. People Locked In
5. Someone Sneezes Over the Food
6. Kitchen Faucet Won't Turn Off

**Roll for Verb:**

1. Preserve
2. Tow
3. Curve
4. Knot
5. Supply
6. Fetch

## ROLL-A-PROMPT WRITING JUMPSTARTS

Character_____
Dilemma_____
Verb_____

CAFETERIA

Character_____
Dilemma_____
Verb_____

ROLL-A-PROMPT WRITING JUMPSTARTS

Character_____
Dilemma_____
Verb_____

CAFETERIA

Character_____
Dilemma_____
Verb_____

ROLL-A-PROMPT WRITING JUMPSTARTS

Character_____
Dilemma_____
Verb_____

## The setting is a Broadway Theater. Write one scene.

**Roll for Character:**

1. Usher
2. Millionaire
3. Toddler
4. Stage Hang
5. Narrator
6. Ticket Cashier

**Roll for Adjective:**

1. Slimy
2. Scintillating
3. Gruesome
4. Thoughtful
5. Mute
6. nonstop

**Roll for Sense:**

1. Knocking
2. Bitter
3. Pungent
4. Rough
5. Goosebumps
6. Sweet

**Roll for Mood:**

- Odd - Tense
- Even - Serine

ROLL-A-PROMPT WRITING JUMPSTARTS

Character_____ Adjective_____
Sense_____Mood_____

BROADWAY THEATER

Character_____ Adjective_____
Sense_____Mood_____

## ROLL-A-PROMPT WRITING JUMPSTARTS

Character_____ Adjective_____
Sense_____Mood_____

BROADWAY THEATER

Character_____ Adjective_____
Sense_____Mood_____

ROLL-A-PROMPT WRITING JUMPSTARTS

Character_____ Adjective_____
Sense_____Mood_____

<u>The setting is a Car Dealership. Write one scene.</u>

**Roll for Character:**

1. Professor
2. Barista
3. Teenager
4. College Student
5. Single Parent
6. Grandparent

**Roll for Dilemma:**

1. Fender Bender
2. Missing Inventory
3. Can't Wake a Customer
4. An Affair is Revealed
5. Embezzlement is Discovered
6. Competition with a Rival

**Roll for Verb:**

1. Gasp
2. Pop
3. Tip
4. Develop
5. Leap
6. Rip

ROLL-A-PROMPT WRITING JUMPSTARTS

Character_____
Dilemma_____
Verb_____

CAR DEALERSHIP

Character_____
Dilemma_____
Verb_____

ROLL-A-PROMPT WRITING JUMPSTARTS

Character_____
Dilemma_____
Verb_____

CAR DEALERSHIP

Character_____
Dilemma_____
Verb_____

## ROLL-A-PROMPT WRITING JUMPSTARTS

Character_____
Dilemma_____
Verb_____

## The setting is an Abandoned Railway Station. Write one scene.

**Roll for Character:**

1. Office Worker
2. Vagabond
3. Teenager
4. Skateboarder
5. Graffiti Artist
6. Real Estate Agent

**Roll for Adjective:**

1. Fascinated
2. Huge
3. Free
4. Third
5. Flimsy
6. Satisfying

**Roll for Sense:**

1. Milky
2. Whisper
3. Shivers
4. Burnt
5. Pitter-Patter
6. Soft

**Roll for Weather:**

- Odd - Clear
- Even - Stormy

## ROLL-A-PROMPT WRITING JUMPSTARTS

Character_____ Adjective_____
Sense_____Weather_____

ABANDONED RAILWAY STATION

Character_____ Adjective_____
Sense_____Weather_____

ROLL-A-PROMPT WRITING JUMPSTARTS

Character_____ Adjective_____
Sense_____Weather_____

ABANDONED RAILWAY STATION

Character_____ Adjective_____
Sense_____Weather_____

## ROLL-A-PROMPT WRITING JUMPSTARTS

Character_____ Adjective_____
Sense_____Weather_____

## The setting is a Bar. Write one scene.

**Roll for Food Choice:**

1. Wings
2. Burgers
3. Popcorn/Bagged Chips
4. Full Menu
5. Fried Only
6. Tapas

**Roll for Bar's Status:**

- Odd - Open
- Even - Closed

**Roll for Word:**

1. Limp
2. Stirrup
3. Damp
4. Precious
5. Asleep
6. Jump

**Roll for Dilemma:**

1. Crying Customer
2. Mysterious Box Arrives
3. Credit Card Rejected
4. Dine N Dash
5. Everyone Starts Singing
6. Blackout

## ROLL-A-PROMPT WRITING JUMPSTARTS

Food_____ Status_____
Word_____ Dilemma_____

BAR

Food_____ Status_____
Word_____ Dilemma_____

## ROLL-A-PROMPT WRITING JUMPSTARTS

Food_____ Status_____
Word_____ Dilemma_____

BAR

Food_____ Status_____
Word_____ Dilemma_____

ROLL-A-PROMPT WRITING JUMPSTARTS

Food_____ Status_____
Word_____ Dilemma_____

## The setting is a Funeral Home. Write one scene.

**Roll for Character:**

1. Embalmer
2. Hearse Driver
3. Usher
4. Pallbearer
5. Grieving Family Member
6. Cosmetologist

**Roll for Dilemma:**

1. Missing Body
2. Inappropriate Note on Flower Arrangement
3. Mourner Confronts Another
4. Halloween Falls on Funeral Service Day
5. Officiant is a No-Show
6. During Service Deceased Repeatedly Called Wrong Name

**Roll for Verb:**

1. Bang
2. Fling
3. Going
4. Beg
5. Shrug
6. Lean

ROLL-A-PROMPT WRITING JUMPSTARTS

Character_____
Dilemma_____
Verb_____

FUNERAL HOME

Character_____
Dilemma_____
Verb_____

ROLL-A-PROMPT WRITING JUMPSTARTS

Character_____
Dilemma_____
Verb_____

FUNERAL HOME

Character_____
Dilemma_____
Verb_____

ROLL-A-PROMPT WRITING JUMPSTARTS

Character_____
Dilemma_____
Verb_____

## The setting is a Cave. Write one scene.

**Roll for Number of MC's Companions.** Use What Comes Up On Your Dice.

**Roll for Line of Dialog:**

1. Are you jealous?
2. I'm not sure why you remember me.
3. Is that a challenge?
4. It's a lullaby.
5. What did you want to tell me?
6. It runs in the family.

**Roll for Verb:**

1. Harass
2. Emboss
3. Cross
4. Diss
5. Guess
6. Press

**Roll for Sense of Danger:**

- Odd - Distinct
- Even - Eminent

ROLL-A-PROMPT WRITING JUMPSTARTS

Companion_____ Dialog_____
Verb_____Danger_____

CAVE

Companion_____ Dialog_____
Verb_____Danger_____

ROLL-A-PROMPT WRITING JUMPSTARTS

Companion_____ Dialog_____
Verb_____Danger_____

CAVE

Companion_____ Dialog_____
Verb_____Danger_____

ROLL-A-PROMPT WRITING JUMPSTARTS

Companion_____ Dialog_____
Verb_____Danger_____

## The setting is an Emergency Room. Write one scene.

**Roll for Character:**

1. Doctor
2. Nurse
3. Orderly
4. Patient
5. Elderly Individual
6. Security Guard

**Roll for Adjective:**

1. Reasonable
2. Kind
3. Abusive
4. Stingy
5. Remarkable
6. Embarrassed

**Roll for Sense:**

1. Whistling
2. Hot
3. Sticky
4. Prickly
5. Refreshing
6. Musty

**Roll for Weather:**

- Odd - Heatwave
- Even - Ice Storm

ROLL-A-PROMPT WRITING JUMPSTARTS

Character_____ Adjective_____
Sense_____Weather_____

EMERGENCY ROOM

Character_____ Adjective_____
Sense_____Weather_____

ROLL-A-PROMPT WRITING JUMPSTARTS

Character_____ Adjective_____
Sense_____Weather_____

EMERGENCY ROOM

Character_____ Adjective_____
Sense_____Weather_____

## ROLL-A-PROMPT WRITING JUMPSTARTS

Character_____ Adjective_____
Sense_____Weather_____

## The setting is a Library. Write one scene.

**Roll for Character:**

1. An Archivist
2. A vagrant
3. An office Supply Delivery Person
4. An Author
5. A Professor
6. A Student

**Roll for Dilemma:**

1. Copy Machine is Generating Random Notes
2. Ceiling is Leaking
3. Several Cell Phones Begin Ringing Incessantly
4. Outside Protest Breaches Door
5. Books from Shelves Disappear
6. There are Tacks All Over the Floor

**Roll for Verb:**

1. Resign
2. Decrease
3. Calculate
4. Stage
5. Embark
6. Fling

## ROLL-A-PROMPT WRITING JUMPSTARTS

Character_____
Dilemma_____
Verb_____

LIBRARY

Character_____
Dilemma_____
Verb_____

## ROLL-A-PROMPT WRITING JUMPSTARTS

Character_____
Dilemma_____
Verb_____

LIBRARY

Character_____
Dilemma_____
Verb_____

## ROLL-A-PROMPT WRITING JUMPSTARTS

Character_____
Dilemma_____
Verb_____

## The setting is a Church Crypt. Write one scene.

**Roll for Time of Day:**

- Odd - Nighttime
- Even - Daytime

**Roll for MC's Companion:**

1. Spouse
2. Arch Nemesis
3. Grandparent
4. First Date
5. Sibling
6. Cab Driver

**Roll for Item:**

1. Fountain Pen
2. Chocolate Bar
3. Baby Food Jar
4. Parasol
5. Watering Can
6. Ukulele

**Roll for Line of Dialog:**

1. It's nothing personal.
2. Rough day today?
3. I'm too trusting.
4. You can't or you won't?
5. I just need to step away for a bit.
6. Promise me?

## ROLL-A-PROMPT WRITING JUMPSTARTS

Time_____Companion_____
Item_____Dialog_____

_____
_____
_____
_____
_____
_____
_____
_____
_____
_____
_____
_____
_____
_____
_____
_____
_____
_____
_____
_____
_____
_____
_____
_____
_____
_____
_____
_____
_____
_____
_____
_____
_____
_____
_____
_____

CHURCH CRYPT

Time_____Companion_____
Item_____Dialog_____

## ROLL-A-PROMPT WRITING JUMPSTARTS

Time_____Companion_____
Item_____Dialog_____

CHURCH CRYPT

Time_____Companion_____
Item_____Dialog_____

ROLL-A-PROMPT WRITING JUMPSTARTS

Time_____Companion_____
Item_____Dialog_____

## The setting is a School Campus. Write one scene.

**Roll for Type:**

- Odd - College
- Even - Boarding School

**Roll for Line of Dialogue:**

1. This has to be closed.
2. Did you hear that?
3. The green ones are tangy.
4. Could you squeeze it?
5. The monkeys have been fed.
6. Why is the air coming out?

**Roll for Item:**

1. Stovetop Popcorn
2. Torch
3. Ballet Shoes
4. Shuttlecock
5. Goggles
6. Hair Pin

**Roll for Number of MC's Companions.** Use What Comes Up On Your Dice.

ROLL-A-PROMPT WRITING JUMPSTARTS

Type_____Dialog_____
Item_____Companions_____

SCHOOL CAMPUS

Type_____Dialog_____
Item_____Companions_____

ROLL-A-PROMPT WRITING JUMPSTARTS

Type_____Dialog_____
Item_____Companions_____

SCHOOL CAMPUS

Type_____Dialog_____
Item_____Companions_____

ROLL-A-PROMPT WRITING JUMPSTARTS

Type_____Dialog_____
Item_____Companions_____

<u>The setting is a Warehouse. Write one scene.</u>

**Roll for MC's Position:**

1. Stocking
2. Payroll
3. Manager
4. Night Supervisor
5. Forklift Driver
6. Maintenance

**Roll for Dilemma:**

1. Shipment Delayed
2. Something Dead is Found
3. Tornado Approaching
4. Phone Line From Unoccupied Office Lights Up On Switchboard
5. Sticky Substance on Floor
6. Loading Dock Doors are Stuck

**Roll for Verb:**

1. Grow
2. Withdraw
3. Borrow
4. Slow
5. Renew
6. View

## ROLL-A-PROMPT WRITING JUMPSTARTS

Position_____ Dilemma_____
Verb_____

A WAREHOUSE

Position_____ Dilemma_____
Verb_____

_____
_____
_____
_____
_____
_____
_____
_____
_____
_____
_____
_____
_____
_____
_____
_____
_____
_____
_____
_____
_____
_____
_____
_____
_____
_____
_____
_____
_____
_____
_____
_____
_____

## ROLL-A-PROMPT WRITING JUMPSTARTS

Position_____ Dilemma_____
Verb_____

A WAREHOUSE

Position_____ Dilemma_____
Verb_____

ROLL-A-PROMPT WRITING JUMPSTARTS

Position_____ Dilemma_____
Verb_____

## The setting is a Camp Site. Write one scene.

**Roll for Style:**

- Odd - Primitive Camping
- Even - Glamorous (Glamping)

**Roll for Activity Available at Site:**

1. Hiking
2. Fishing
3. Canoe
4. Zip-line
5. Archery
6. No Extra Activities

**Roll for Reason to go Camping:**

1. Divorce
2. Wedding
3. Reunion
4. Graduation
5. End of Summer
6. Beginning of Summer

**Roll for Verb:**

1. Gallop
2. Drip
3. Harp
4. Tamp
5. Warp
6. Eavesdrop

## ROLL-A-PROMPT WRITING JUMPSTARTS

Style_____ Activity_____
Reason_____Verb_____

CAMP SITE

Style_____ Activity_____
Reason_____Verb_____

## ROLL-A-PROMPT WRITING JUMPSTARTS

Style_____ Activity_____
Reason_____Verb_____

CAMP SITE

Style_____ Activity_____
Reason_____Verb_____

## ROLL-A-PROMPT WRITING JUMPSTARTS

Style_____ Activity_____
Reason_____Verb_____

## The setting is a Nightclub. Write one scene.

**Roll for Time:**

- Odd - Lunchtime
- Even - After Midnight

**Roll for Theme:**

1. Fifties
2. Tropical
3. Punk
4. Cabaret
5. Drag King
6. Speakeasy

**Roll for Sense:**

1. Slippery
2. Matted
3. Pitch Black
4. Velvety
5. Dagger
6. Spicy

**Roll for Adverb:**

1. Anxious
2. Majestical
3. Obnoxious
4. Inquisitive
5. Dim
6. Boastful

ROLL-A-PROMPT WRITING JUMPSTARTS

Time_____Theme_____
Sense_____Adverb_____

NIGHTCLUB

Time_____Theme_____
Sense_____Adverb_____

ROLL-A-PROMPT WRITING JUMPSTARTS

Time_____Theme_____
Sense_____Adverb_____

NIGHTCLUB

Time_____Theme_____
Sense_____Adverb_____

## ROLL-A-PROMPT WRITING JUMPSTARTS

Time_____Theme_____
Sense_____Adverb_____

## The setting is a Cooking Class. Write one scene.

**Roll for MC's Full-time Job:**

1. Electrician
2. Farmer
3. Pool Cleaner
4. Tailor
5. Horticulturalist
6. Deep Sea Diver

**Roll for Dilemma:**

1. Timer Doesn't Go Off
2. Air Conditioner Malfunctions
3. No Labels on Spice Rack
4. Your Assignment Partner Has No sense of Taste
5. The Class Next Door is Noisy
6. An Ex is the Teacher

**Roll for Verb:**

1. Fall
2. Seal
3. Cancel
4. Entail
5. Fulfill
6. Spoil

## ROLL-A-PROMPT WRITING JUMPSTARTS

Job_____
Dilemma_____
Verb_____

COOKING CLASS

Job_____
Dilemma_____
Verb_____

## ROLL-A-PROMPT WRITING JUMPSTARTS

Job_____
Dilemma_____
Verb_____

COOKING CLASS

Job_____
Dilemma_____
Verb_____

## ROLL-A-PROMPT WRITING JUMPSTARTS

Job_____
Dilemma_____
Verb_____

## The setting is a Nursing Home. Write one scene.

**Roll for Character:**

1. Pharmaceutical Rep
2. Health Aide
3. New Resident
4. Billing Clerk
5. Front Desk
6. Cafeteria Worker

**Roll for Adjective:**

1. Agreeable
2. Well-off
3. Scientific
4. Elated
5. Smiling
6. Wacky

**Roll for Holiday:**

1. St. Patrick's Day
2. Fourth of July
3. Memorial Day
4. Groundhog Day
5. Veteran's Day
6. Summer Solstice

**Roll for Entertainment:**

- Odd - Musical
- Even - Magic

ROLL-A-PROMPT WRITING JUMPSTARTS

Character_____ Adjective_____
Holiday_____Entertainment_____

NURSING HOME

Character_____ Adjective_____
Holiday_____Entertainment_____

ROLL-A-PROMPT WRITING JUMPSTARTS

Character_____ Adjective_____
Holiday_____Entertainment_____

NURSING HOME

Character_____ Adjective_____
Holiday_____Entertainment_____

ROLL-A-PROMPT WRITING JUMPSTARTS

Character_____ Adjective_____
Holiday_____Entertainment_____

**Roll-A-Prompt Writing Series**

**Genre Editions:**

- Mystery
- Horror
- Sci-Fi
- Romance
- Fantasy
- Genre Mashup
- More Coming 2023

**Story Building Editions:**

- Conflict
- Scene
- Five Senses
- More Coming 2023

For updates on new Roll-A-Prompt Writing Journals and periodic live writing prompt sessions, join our community when you download your free PDF worksheets at: https://BookHip.com/FZHMZA

Made in United States
Troutdale, OR
12/30/2023